WHY DOES MY
DOG
Lick Me?

This edition reprinted in 2017
by Baker & Taylor UK Ltd
Bicester, Oxfordshire OX26 4ST

© Susanna Geoghegan Gift Publishing

Illustrations © Irisz Agocs
Contents layout: seagulls.net
Author: Michael Powell
Cover design: Milestone Creative

ISBN: 978-1-910562-34-5

Printed in China

CONTENTS

INTRODUCTION

DOGS ARE AMAZING, BUT THEY'RE ALSO
UNFATHOMABLE, EVEN THOUGH MANY OF US
THINK WE KNOW EXACTLY WHAT THEY WANT
AND WHAT THEY ARE FEELING OR THINKING.

The reality is that although they have learned to live with
humans since we were hunter-gatherers, we increasingly
ignore that dogs are from a different species with unique
body language, sensory equipment, social cues and
survival imperatives. In short, if you think you know your
dog, you are greatly mistaken.

Dogs are expert at reading our body language and
facial expressions but most of us are woefully inept at

understanding their preoccupations and complex needs. Dogs communicate their feelings and requirements but we just need to learn how to see into their world and recognize how their heightened senses, instinct and genetic inheritance form an important part of their psychological makeup.

Sometimes we just need to take ourselves out of the equation. For example, if your dog follows you around, this behaviour is more likely caused by under-stimulation and insecurity than hero-worship. Get over it – you're not that interesting. More than anything dogs like order in their pack. It's your job as the alpha to create the perfect dog-friendly home environment of stability, calmness and predictable routine, and the foundation for all of this is effective communication.

Dogs are extraordinary because they agree to share our homes, on our terms, and they make the most compromises; the least we can do is to pay them the attention and respect that they deserve. So this book answers forty-five of the most commonly asked questions about canine behaviour. Understanding how your dog communicates is a vital part of enjoying a happy and healthy friend.

Stealing
SOCKS

PETTY THIEVERY IS ONE OF THE MORE ANNOYING
CANINE TRAITS, BUT LIKE MOST BEHAVIOUR IT GIVES
YOU CLUES ABOUT HOW YOUR DOG IS FEELING.

In the case of stealing, your dog is probably feeling bored,
ignored and under-stimulated. So if you're fed up with
retrieving your personal belongings from all corners of the
house and garden (in the rain), you can interrupt the habit
even if you can't eliminate it completely.

Reaction

When your dog steals a sock, your reaction is reward enough, even scolding (because negative attention is still attention). If you shout and wrestle the item away from him, it can either turn into an amusing tug of war that reinforces the behaviour (and your dog has succeeded in getting you to play with him) or your anger can be a confusing and even frightening experience that increases his anxiety and loneliness. The best reaction is to quietly retrieve the object when your dog has lost interest; if the item is dangerous or about to get chewed to pieces, use a distraction such as a play toy (not food, otherwise he will quickly learn that he can get a treat every time he steals

something). Don't shout and scold because he probably won't connect your shouting with the stealing behaviour.

The best way to reduce sock theft is to prevent access (tidy up your house – put things away), provide 'legal' alternatives such as chew toys and give your dog more attention, exercise and mental stimulation.

Kicking Its Leg During A
TUMMY RUB

LOTS OF DOGS LOVE HAVING THEIR BELLIES RUBBED BUT MANY LITERALLY GET A KICK OUT OF IT – THEIR LEG STARTS WHIRRING IN AN INVOLUNTARY SCRATCHING ACTION THAT RARELY MAKES CONTACT WITH THEIR SKIN AND OFTEN SEEMS TO BEMUSE THE DOG AS MUCH AS IT AMUSES ITS OWNER. HOWEVER, IT IS A SIGN OF IRRITATION SO DON'T MAKE IT A PARTY PIECE.

Irritant

When you scratch a dog's tummy, the nerves in that region sense an irritant, which could be an insect or parasite, or some other unwanted stimulation. In this case it's your hand but the nerve impulses travel up the spine to the brain just the same and tell the leg to scratch to remove the potential threat (like a bug carrying disease). In this respect it's an indication of irritation so you shouldn't really try to make it happen too often. Move onto another part of the belly or flank until the leg kicking stops.

Scratch reflex

Dogs that are already prone to allergies are more likely to show the scratch reflex because their nervous system is more highly attuned to irritants. Vets also use this belly rub kicking reflex to test for neurological problems, much like a doctor checks a patient's reflexes by tapping the knee to make the leg jerk. Bad reflexes are a sign of illness. The scratch reflex is also very similar to the way humans and other animals respond to painful stimuli – our limbs automatically jerk away from pain without us having to consciously think about it.

TEARING
Things Up

MOST DOGS LOVE TO CHEW AND RIP THINGS APART
BUT WHEN THE HABIT BECOMES EXCESSIVE AND
DAMAGES YOUR PROPERTY, IT'S TIME TO HELP
CHANGE THE BEHAVIOUR – NOT ONLY TO PROTECT
YOUR STUFF, BUT, MOST IMPORTANT OF ALL,
TO CARE FOR YOUR DOG.

If your dog tears up soft furnishings, paper, shoes etc. while she is home alone, it's a sign that she is bored and anxious. Even if she does it when you're in the house, it means that she has too much energy and needs more exercise and attention.

A little bit of tearing is fun and it helps to clean her teeth and stimulate the jaw and gums, but even if you don't mind clearing up the mess, don't use your tolerance threshold as the place to act – think about your dog's wellbeing much earlier.

Exercise

Dogs need plenty of physical and mental exercise. If you are going to be out for a few hours, try to walk the dog first or spend ten minutes playing. This should delay any anxiety and boredom issues while you are out because the endorphins generated by the exercise will take at least an hour to wear off.

The other obvious preventative measure is to remove items that are likely to be chewed – for example, put shoes away in a cupboard, and don't leave magazines lying around at dog level. If exercise doesn't reduce the unwanted chewing, you may have to confine your dog to a single 'dog-proofed' room while you're out, to break the repetitive cycle.

Moving Away From My HUGS

IF YOUR DOG MOVES AWAY FROM YOUR HUGS THEN IT MEANS THAT IN COMMON WITH MOST OTHER MEMBERS OF THE SPECIES, HE DOESN'T MUCH LIKE THEM.

Believe it or not, hugging is not normal canine behaviour. Dogs may lie close to one another but they don't grab each other by the neck and hold each other close, and they tend to find face-to-face contact threatening. Child hugs – grabbing the dog tightly around the neck and forcing heads close together – is a major cause of bites because many dogs interpret this behaviour as aggressive and react in kind.

You might protest that your dog is different and loves cuddles and even lies on top of you demanding close contact. If your dog asks for this kind of affection on his own terms, then all well and good, but in many cases dogs simply learn to tolerate hugs and remain still until the unpleasantness stops.

So the most important rule for dog hugs is always to invite the dog and not to pull him close to you for a big squeezy hug against his will. Just because he doesn't stop you doesn't mean he's having fun. Don't be selfish and assume your dog is having the best time simply because it makes you feel good. Always give him the space to walk away so he doesn't feel trapped or coerced. If you have a tiny dog, it is even more important that you respect his personal space and don't keep picking him up to satisfy your own hugging requirements!

PULLING
On Its Leash

IF YOUR DOG PULLS ON HER LEASH IT IS BECAUSE SHE HAS LEARNED THAT WHEN SHE SEES SOMETHING INTERESTING, SHE CAN GET THERE MORE QUICKLY BY WALKING FASTER AND PULLING YOU ALONG.

She's not trying to become pack leader by reaching the front; she's not even trying to challenge your authority; she doesn't have to because you already made her the boss long ago, the first time you allowed her to get what she wanted by pulling. You have taught her that pulling works. You did that.

The best way to teach your dog that pulling is a waste of time is to stop every time she pulls, hold the leash against your navel and quietly and calmly wait for her to release the tension on the leash before you continue. Every time. She pulls, you stop and wait for her to take a few steps back towards you. No matter how long it takes, she doesn't get to move again until the leash is loose. If she's been pulling for a long time, it will take a long time to break the habit, so don't give up after five minutes, or one walk. It may take several weeks to teach the new rule.

You must be one hundred per cent consistent. Just one lapse will teach your dog that pulling works eventually, undoing hours of good training. Even more damaging, it will teach you that your training method doesn't work, and you will quickly spiral into self-doubt, your dog will pull more often and you will eventually abandon the training and blame everything but yourself.

KICKING GRASS
After Peeing

DOGS SCRAPE THE GROUND AFTER DOING THEIR BUSINESS FOR THE EXACT OPPOSITE REASON TO CATS. CATS LIKE TO BURY AND CONCEAL WHERE THEY HAVE BEEN BUT DOGS LIKE TO ADVERTISE AND MARK THEIR TERRITORY, ALTHOUGH THE SCRAPING SERVES TO ACTIVATE SCENT GLANDS AS WELL AS SPREAD THE ACTUAL SMELL OF THEIR BUSINESS.

Dogs have scent glands underneath their paws and between their toes. Scraping the ground transfers their unique scent next to their business to proudly announce, 'I did this!' You might consider this excessive, since urine and faeces are pungent enough, but actually the doggy scent lasts longer because their business becomes less smelly once it dries out. The deep scrape marks left in the ground also provide a visual clue to the size, strength and dominance of the dog.

Dogs cock their legs against trees and other vertical surfaces to satisfy the same urge to advertise: the higher up they can pee, the greater the area covered, the more of the lower scents from other dogs are obscured and the further their scent will travel in the air.

This behaviour is perfectly normal. In fact, if your dog is a habitual ground scraper but suddenly stops, this may be an indication of pain caused by arthritis or some other complaint that reduces mobility. Scratching is also a sign of your dog's actual or perceived position in the local canine pecking order. This behaviour is most frequently observed in dogs that consider themselves to be dominant.

Chasing its TAIL

DOGS ARE AT THEIR FUNNIEST WHEN THEY'RE CHASING THEIR TAILS. IT'S THE EPITOME OF POINTLESS REPETITIVE BEHAVIOUR AND IT ALWAYS MAKES PEOPLE LAUGH BECAUSE IT LOOKS LIKE THE DOG HAS NO IDEA THAT HIS TAIL IS PART OF HIS OWN BODY; EVEN IF HE DOES, IT'S STILL FUNNY HOW SIMPLY HE CAN AMUSE HIMSELF. AH, TO BE SO EASILY SATISFIED. A TAIL-CHASING DOG IS ALMOST TO BE ENVIED.

Actually, it's not a healthy behaviour and it should be discouraged. Dogs chase their tails for a variety of reasons, but all of them need tackling. It's usually a solitary pastime. Dogs don't chase their tails when they are stimulated and in the company of other dogs. So it can be a warning sign of stress, boredom or loneliness. When your dog chases his tail, don't just stand there laughing. Play with him or take him for a walk and give him more opportunities to socialize with other dogs.

Other possible causes of tail chasing, and especially tail chewing, are fleas, ticks and worms. Your dog can find temporary relief by chewing. It's a displacement activity. Check also for matted tail hair which can cause irritation and restrict blood flow if it becomes severe. Brush your dog regularly to remove dirt, spread natural oils throughout the coat and to check for flea dust.

Obsessive tail chasing needs urgent intervention. Divert attention away from the unwanted activity and redirect your dog into more positive activities. Once you have resolved all of these possible causes, the unhealthy tail chasing will cease.

YAWNING
When Not Sleepy

YAWNING IS A FASCINATING PIECE OF CANINE BODY LANGUAGE THAT CAN HELP TO DIFFUSE CONFLICT AND IS ALSO USED BY DOGS TO PACIFY THEIR OWNERS. OBSERVATION OF CANINE BEHAVIOUR HAS SHOWN THAT DOGS ARE MORE LIKELY TO YAWN WHEN THEY ARE UNDER STRESS.

A dog will often yawn directly after it has been scolded by its owner. If you have ever attended a badly run dog obedience class in which owners are allowed to loudly shout commands at their dogs, you will have witnessed this yawning response first hand. A dog will 'stay', apparently calmly in response to its owner's excessive instructions, then perform a large yawn, or sometimes a half yawn.

Dogs yawn to express their uncertainty in response to stress, but they also break eye contact, turn their head away and then yawn to pacify other dogs, although it isn't a sign of submission. Often you'll see a dominant dog yawn in response to aggressive behaviour such as growling from a dog who is feeling anxious and under threat. After the yawn the aggressive dog visibly relaxes and may initiate normal greeting behaviour.

You can also turn your head away and yawn to put a strange dog at its ease, especially in situations where it is difficult for you to physically move away.

If your dog yawns while you are petting her, this could be a polite way of asking you to stop. The best way to check whether your dog wants you to continue is to stop petting and then see if she tries to get you to restart the petting (such as by nuzzling your hand with her head, moving closer, flopping onto you). If she doesn't want to be petted she will turn or duck her head away, lick her lips, move away, or simply yawn.

Sticking Its Head Out Of The
CAR
WINDOW

AN OLD JOKE MAKES THE OBSERVATION
THAT DOGS HATE ANYONE BLOWING IN THEIR
FACES BUT CAN'T RESIST STICKING THEIR
HEADS OUT OF A MOVING VEHICLE.

There's no scientific evidence regarding why dogs enjoy the wind in their hair, but several dog behaviourists agree that the attraction may be connected to their sense of smell rather than any other sensory experience.

Dogs have about 250 million smell receptors in their noses compared to about 5 million in humans. Air passes over a structure inside the nose called the olfactory membrane. Ours is the size of a postage stamp; a dog's is the size of an envelope. The more air that passes over the membrane,

the more smells it can detect, so when a dog travels in a car the volume of air passing over the membrane must be almost overwhelming.

Cooling down

However, there are additional attractions: the feeling of wind in the face is exhilarating and is a good way to cool down during a hot journey; also dogs do like to watch the world whizz by as well as smell it.

Unfortunately, wind surfing should be discouraged for the same reason that children should be prevented from craning their necks out of the car window: they can jump out or get injured if you brake suddenly, they can get grit and insects in their eyes, ears and mouths, and too much wind can cause problems inside the ear canal. Even breathing in the air at such high velocity can damage a dog's lungs.

SUCKING
Its Blanket

CHEWING IS NORMAL DOG BEHAVIOUR.
SUCKING IN ADULT DOGS IS USUALLY ASSOCIATED
WITH THEIR EXPERIENCE AS A PUPPY. PUPPIES
NATURALLY SEEK OUT THEIR MOTHER'S MILK
AND GAIN VALUABLE NUTRITION AND COMFORT
FROM SUCKLING SESSIONS, WHICH THE
MOTHER USUALLY ALLOWS FOR UP TO
TWO MONTHS AFTER BIRTH.

Primary reflex

Suckling is called a 'primary reflex' because it doesn't have to be taught. Newborn puppies also have a burrowing reflex which makes them seek out the warmth of the mother's fur and snuggle in. If the puppy can't immediately satisfy these needs (in a large litter puppies have to compete for their turn on the teat) he will satisfy the reflex by sucking on a nearby blanket.

So long as the puppy's suckling and burrowing needs are consistently met, the blanket sucking behaviour will not become a habit; but if a puppy is weaned too early or is one of the submissive members of the litter, he may have to resort to this self-comforting behaviour often until it becomes an ingrained habit.

Some breeds are genetically more prone to blanket sucking, such as Doberman Pinschers and Dachshunds. If your adult dog is a blanket sucker it's not a major cause for concern, but it can be a useful indicator of the times when he is feeling insecure and needs comfort. When you observe this behaviour, make his immediate environment calmer and more secure and remove anything that could be triggering his anxiety.

Licking Its
NOSE

A DOG LICKING ITS NOSE LOOKS IMPOSSIBLY CUTE TO HUMANS BUT IT'S AN IMPORTANT CALMING MECHANISM AND PIECE OF DOG VOCABULARY.

A lick of the nose occurs most frequently during moments of uncertainty. When a dog faces a demanding or confusing situation, it may perform this movement while it decides how to react.

So nose licking is a sign that your dog is weighing up a situation and also expresses a certain amount of anxiety, but it is not a cause for concern, since it also shows that the dog is self-soothing, staying relatively calm while she considers her options.

Humans employ similar absent-minded self-touching gestures at times of mental conflict. We scratch our heads when confused to help us focus and stay relaxed while we wrestle with a knotty problem. We may feel anxiety, frustration and even mild anger, but a head scratch is rarely an aggressive gesture and the same applies to nose licking.

Dogs often lick their noses to steel their resolve just before they approach an unfamiliar dog. Some experts believe the gesture also helps to calm other dogs by communicating that the uncertainty is being contained without the need to escalate the situation to violence.

If your dog licks her nose at you, it may be a sign that you need to communicate your wishes and commands more clearly and/or calmly.

PRESSING
Its Head Against The
WALL

HEAD PRESSING OCCURS WHEN AN ANIMAL STANDS FACING A WALL OR ANOTHER HARD SURFACE (DOOR, SOFA) AND THEN PRESSES THE TOP OF ITS HEAD AGAINST IT.

If you ever witness this behaviour (even if the animal is standing facing the wall or a corner, without the pressing) take your dog to the vet immediately because it is usually a sign of serious illness – a medical emergency requiring immediate treatment and probably hospitalization. However, many of the causes can be treated and the animal can make a full recovery if diagnosed and treated quickly.

The most common prognosis for compulsive head pressing is damage to the nervous system, commonly caused by prosencephalon disease (in which the forebrain and thalamus parts of the brain are damaged) or toxins, including liver failure blood poisoning which causes the accumulation in the bloodstream of toxins that are normally removed by a healthy liver. Other causes include head trauma, brain tumours or a metabolic disorder such as hyper- or hyponatremia (too much, or too little sodium in the blood plasma), stroke, rabies, fungal infection, hydrocephalus (water on the brain that causes acute pain as it presses against the inside of the skull).

Other symptoms

Head pressing may be one of the more obvious symptoms of the serious conditions listed above, but you should also be aware that the following behaviours could also be indicative: walking in circles; pacing anxiously and aimlessly; irregular reflexes; tremors and shaking; seizures and visual impairment.

Please note that head pressing is not the same as head butting or rubbing, where your animal presses up against you and butts or brushes his head against your leg or another part of your body. This is normal healthy doggy attention-seeking behaviour.

Looking GUILTY

YOU RETURN HOME, YOU OPEN THE FRONT DOOR
AND SPOT A CHEWED CUSHION IN THE HALL.
INSTEAD OF THE CUSTOMARY EXCITED GREETING
YOUR DOG IS EITHER HIDING OR IS IN NO
HURRY TO MEET YOUR GAZE.

Your hackles immediately rise and you call her name suspiciously, and right on cue, as if to confirm your suspicions, she slinks in, tail between her legs. Her hindquarters are low, her head is bowed, she blinks softly and licks her nose. 'What have you done?' you probe with an inquisitorial tone. By now your dog's eyes are nearly closed and she looks like she wants to melt into the wall. Is she really expressing guilt?

Guilt is a very sophisticated emotion and well beyond the intellectual capacity of any dog. However, she is an expert at reading your body language and the tone of your voice.

Caution

As soon as you begin to suspect that something is wrong, your behaviour will change and your dog will sense this and react accordingly. If you sound angry or even mildly accusatory, your dog will know that this is not a usual entrance. She will hold back, show caution and study you with rapt attention for further visual and auditory clues.

Submissive

Your dog is not showing guilt; she is adopting a submissive posture in response to your atypical homecoming. She won't know that you are cross about her chewing the cushion three hours ago. She will see you pointing and frowning but she won't make the connection. All she knows is the anger is directed towards her, so she follows the evolutionary imperative to placate you.

STARING *At Me*

WHEN YOUR DOG STARES AT YOU IT'S USUALLY A GOOD SIGN – HE'S ENGAGING DIRECTLY WITH YOU, HIS WONDERFUL OWNER, WHOM HE LOVES UNCONDITIONALLY. THERE'S NOTHING BETTER THAN RECEIVING A PROLONGED ADORING GAZE FROM YOUR BEST FRIEND. TRAINERS ENCOURAGE THEIR DOGS TO WATCH THEM ATTENTIVELY, ALERT AND READY FOR THE NEXT COMMAND.

However, the most likely explanation is that he wants something. It could be a treat, it might be time for dinner. He might want you to follow him to the back door so you can let him outside to have a pee. If he comes to find you and then stands or sits staring, he definitely wants something, so if you're busy don't just brush him off and send him away with a quick pat. Try to find out what he wants, so that he's encouraged to communicate his needs more often. If you are in the habit of ignoring these kinds of interactions, he will quickly learn to his chagrin that his owner simply isn't very responsive and you will have lost another opportunity to bond and strengthen mutual affection and trust. After all, you expect your dog to pay attention to you, so it's only fair to return the favour.

Love and attachment

According to a recent article in the journal *Science*, a prolonged stare from a dog can sometimes simply be a sign of love and attachment to its owner. A team of Japanese researchers recorded elevated levels of the hormone oxytocin (associated with nurturing and attachment) in both dogs' and owners' brains as a result of maintaining eye contact.

This privileged bond is based on trust and familiarity, so don't under any circumstances stare at a strange dog because the animal will perceive it as a direct challenge.

Getting Excited By
VISITORS

EVEN THE MOST DOCILE DOG CAN TURN INTO A BARKING, JUMPING, FRENZIED DEVIL WHEN GUESTS ARRIVE. IT'S NATURAL FOR A DOG TO REACT TO NEW STIMULI, AND NEW PEOPLE AND NEW SMELLS ENTERING THE HOUSE CAN BE A SOURCE OF GREAT DELIGHT FOR YOUR DOG.

In some cases it's so bad that the dog can stop any of the humans interacting with each other for a good twenty minutes or so while they focus on getting it to settle down.

Ignore the dog

All your guests see when they visit you is a badly behaved, out-of-control and rather annoying animal, no matter how much you protest that your dog is no trouble at all when there are no visitors.

Sometimes, being a responsible dog owner involves getting other people to cooperate – you have to instruct humans as well as your dog! The best way to prevent this behaviour is to ask your guests to ignore the dog when they first arrive, so that she isn't rewarded for jumping up, skidding around the room, barking and generally being a nuisance. She needs to learn that she will be rewarded with attention only when the humans are ready to give it and only if she is being calm and well behaved. The golden rule is always to ignore unwanted behaviour and to praise and reward desirable behaviour.

However, this approach will only work if you have done lots of training beforehand on teaching her to sit and stay when the doorbell rings, or when someone comes through the front door. After several weeks of rehearsing good behaviour and rewarding with treats, she will soon associate visitors with sitting quietly – it simply becomes the thing that she does, rather than tearing around the house barking and jumping all over your guests.

Turning Its BACK

SOMETIMES YOUR DOG WILL GREET YOU, THEN AS YOU REACH DOWN TO STROKE HIS HEAD OR TICKLE HIS EARS, HE WILL TURN AROUND, LEAN IN TO YOU AND PRESENT HIS BACKSIDE, WHILE TURNING HIS HEAD TO LOOK BACK ADORINGLY OVER HIS SHOULDER AT YOU, WITH HIS EARS BACK.

This isn't simply a sign that he feels relaxed and happy with you. He is probably inviting you to rub the base of his tail.

Many dogs like having the base of their tails scratched and rubbed (although some hate it, so pay attention to your dog's body language and don't force a back rub on a dog who keeps walking away or whips its head round quickly).

Hard to reach

Their pleasure in having a back rub is no big mystery – humans like having their backs scratched too so we can appreciate the simple satisfaction of attending to an area that is hard to reach. The base of the tail is out of reach of a dog's paws (they may have a good try with their teeth, although that requires considerable contortion).

Be vigilant

If your dog asks you to scratch his back more than usual, take a look at the area to check for skin irritation as well as fleas, ticks and mites. Or he might have an allergy to pesticides, mould or pollen, so as always, stay vigilant to any changes in his behaviour and take him to the vet if you have any concerns. Otherwise, enjoy giving him a good back rub and take pleasure in that blissful and contented look on his face. You aren't imagining it.

Loving An
EAR RUB

MOST DOGS LIKE NOTHING BETTER THAN A REALLY GOOD EAR RUB. YOUR DOG'S PLEASURE IS TANGIBLE WHEN YOU GENTLY CUP HER HEAD IN YOUR HANDS AND THEN REACH BEHIND HER EARS WITH YOUR FINGERTIPS TO DELIVER A LITTLE PIECE OF HEAVEN.

Your dog responds by closing her eyes, lifting her chin slightly and even deep breathing and snorting with sheer pleasure. But why is an ear rub such a big deal?

The answer is very simple: the area around a dog's ears contains a dense network of nerve fibres (as does her belly and between her toes) that is very sensitive to touch. Rubbing stimulates these nerves as well as the pituitary and hypothalamus glands, which releases endorphins into the bloodstream. It also relaxes the neck muscles and encourages better blood flow in that area. You can experience a similar relaxation by massaging behind your own ears and gently pulling on your ear lobes. It's a natural sedative for dog and owner. Studies show that rubbing your dog's ears can reduce your blood pressure and encourage the release of your own feel-good chemicals.

Dominance

However, there is another important component to the ear rub that is often overlooked. When you place your hands on a dog's head you are showing your dominance, which is why a strange dog will react less favourably to your uninvited bonding session. So when you meet a new dog, show a bit of respect, courtesy and restraint rather than diving straight in for what will prove to be a rather disappointing ear rub that will leave the poor animal feeling anxious and rudely handled.

COCKING Its Head

HUMANS FIND HEAD COCKING ONE OF THE MOST SATISFYING OF ALL DOGGY GESTURES. IT NOT ONLY LOOKS CUTE, BUT IT MAKES US FEEL SUPER SPECIAL TO BE THE OBJECT OF SUCH RAPT ATTENTION.

In fact, thousands of years of interaction between our two species indicate that the head tilt is a very sophisticated response with several imperatives.

Firstly, the muscles that control the dog's inner ear also control facial expression and head movements, so this may be a fine-tuning gesture that helps the dog to better pinpoint the precise location of a sound. Tilting the head makes the ear more exposed in an up-and-forward position, so it can pick up sounds more precisely.

Seeing clearly

However, this isn't the whole story because there's also an important visual component. Dogs continually scan our faces for information. Recent research suggests that head tilting may also help your dog to see your mouth more clearly. Dog sensory perception expert Dr Stanley Coren has a theory that dogs with longer noses cock their heads more frequently than breeds with flatter faces such as Pugs, Boston Terriers and Pekingese. He conducted an online survey with 582 participants and found a statistically significant correlation between muzzle size and head tilting. If you hold your fist up to your nose, you'll notice that tilting your head allows you to see someone's mouth more clearly, so this visual component is definitely an important factor.

When you are talking directly to your dog, the head tilt demonstrates that the dog is listening, trying to pick up cues in your tone of voice, or listening out for key words that mean something good or exciting is about to happen. However, if you reinforce this 'cute' behaviour with praise or fuss, your dog may simply have learned that doing this brings rewards and may just do it for effect!

Drinking From The
TOILET

NOTHING PUTS YOU OFF GETTING AFFECTIONATE
LICKS FROM YOUR DOG MORE THAN THE SIGHT OF HER
DRINKING ENTHUSIASTICALLY FROM THE TOILET BOWL.

First you are hit with a pang of guilt, because you assume that the water bowl in the kitchen is less appealing to her than the toilet; then you come to your senses and face the grim truth that sometimes dogs can just be plain disgusting. But actually, it's partly your fault.

Dogs love to drink fresh, preferably running water that is cool and well oxygenated. If your dog's regular water bowl has been sitting in a warm kitchen for several hours it will need freshening up if you want to keep her out of the bathroom. The water in the toilet bowl is cool and refreshing. Unfortunately it's also teeming with bacteria and potentially harmful cleaning chemicals like bleach, so drinking it is definitely to be discouraged. The best way is to close the lid and the bathroom door.

Now get to work on providing several sources of fresh, cool drinking water. Place two or three bowls around the house and change the water several times a day. Use porcelain bowls rather than plastic, which can leach chemicals and is harder to keep bacteria free. Every evening, clean the bowls with hot water and a little washing up liquid and rinse well. On a hot summer's day, drop a few ice cubes into the drinking bowls for a refreshing treat.

HOWLING
At Opera

DOGS DON'T NEED MUCH ENCOURAGEMENT TO LAUNCH INTO A FULL-BLOWN SOULFUL HOWL. MUSIC THAT CONTAINS HIGH-PITCHED SOPRANOS OR INSTRUMENTS SUCH AS THE CLARINET, PIANO OR SAXOPHONE CAN EASILY SET THEM OFF. OTHER COMMON ENVIRONMENTAL HOWLING TRIGGERS INCLUDE AMBULANCE, POLICE, OR FIRE ENGINE SIRENS. THEY AREN'T JUST KEEPING THE BLUES ALIVE; THEY ARE RESPONDING TO THEIR ANCESTRAL URGE TO COMMUNICATE WITH THE PACK.

Disconcerting

It is common knowledge that wolves howl to contact separated members of their pack, reinforce their strong social bonds and rally the pack before hunting, but did you know that all wolves howl in the key of E, the same as whales and dolphins? So the next time your dog starts howling to a piece of music, find out what key the piece is written in. It's probably less relevant than the pitch, but still worth recording the experiment.

It can be disconcerting to witness your pet howling at music, because stripped of a normal context such as pain, separation anxiety, boundary demarcation or an expression of anxiety, the dog often appears confused and sends us other messages of high arousal such as a wagging tail and panting. It looks like the dog is having an unpleasant experience, not least because of the heart-wrenching moan erupting from his very core, but there's no harm done, so long as you allow him an escape route (i.e. keep the door open, so he can leave the room to get away from the stimulus) and don't allow him to remain in this highly aroused state for very long.

Rolling In
MUCK

DOGS HAVE A CURIOUS AND OFTEN EXASPERATING
AFFINITY FOR ROLLING IN THE RANKEST PILE OF
MUCK THEY CAN FIND. BUT IT DOESN'T STOP AT
HORSE APPLES OR STINKY BADGER DROPPINGS.
THEY'LL HAPPILY CROWN A PLEASANT OUTING
TO THE BEACH BY ANOINTING THEMSELVES
WITH THE SCENT OF DEAD FISH.

Pat Goodmann, research associate and curator of Wolf Park in Indiana, has extensively studied scent rolling among the wolf population and has discovered that a wide variety of strong odours can be good candidates for rolling. The wolves were presented with a selection of smells and rolled in many of them, including Old Spice aftershave, fly repellent, mint extract and Chanel No. 5. They didn't restrict themselves to unpleasant odours.

Once the smell has been transferred to the side of their face and neck they return home where they are greeted and smelled by the rest of the pack, sharing this important information, which could relate to prey, predators and other environmental data vital for survival.

Another plausible reason for rolling is to disguise the dog's own smell, so they can get closer to their prey without detection. This behaviour has been observed widely throughout the animal and plant kingdom.

So the wolf doesn't roll in the scent purely for its own pleasure. It does so because this is the most efficient way to record the message that they will carry to the rest of the pack: 'Check out this awesome food source/disguise'.

Licking And Chewing Its
FEET

THERE ARE FEW THINGS GUARANTEED TO DRIVE YOU INSANE MORE EFFECTIVELY THAN THE NOCTURNAL SOUND OF YOUR DOG OBSESSIVELY LICKING HER PAWS.

Although compulsive scratching and licking behaviours are quite common in dogs, try to figure out the cause. Take your dog to the vet if the problem persists, especially if you can see areas of swelling and bleeding or if your dog is limping or in pain.

Pigments

The first thing you'll notice, especially if she has light-coloured fur, is that the affected area is pink or rusty-coloured. This isn't necessarily blood or sore skin. The colour is often the result of the porphyrin pigments in her saliva, so it can look nastier and more painful than it actually is.

Irritants

Licking can be an indication of a variety of complaints, including cuts on the toes or paw pads, broken claws, corns, or small irritants stuck between the toes (stones, burrs, splinters, shards of glass). Grass seeds can commonly penetrate the skin and lodge themselves deeper and deeper, between tendons and ligaments, and in extreme cases even move up to the shoulder or the groin. It's a good idea to get into the habit of checking your dog's paws, especially between her toes, after a walk.

Another common cause of excessive paw chewing is a skin problem due to allergies. Be alert to recent changes in your dog's environment in and around your home, as well as her diet. A new piece of furniture or carpet may contain chemicals that cause her irritation. Also consider whether you have planted anything new in the garden or if she is being exposed to anything new on her walks. Finally, don't neglect parasites. Is her flea and tick treatment up to date?

Once you've spoken to your vet and ruled out all physical causes, you might conclude that your dog is anxious and bored – the solution is, as always, more exercise, attention, petting and play.

Loving SNOW

MOST DOGS LOVE BOUNDING AROUND IN THE SNOW AND APPEAR TO BE AS GENUINELY EXCITED BY THE CARPET OF WHITE AS WE ARE, ESPECIALLY IN PARTS OF THE WORLD WHERE BLANKET SNOWFALL IS A RARE OCCURRENCE.

So why do they get so excited, when they don't get a day off school and all the interesting smells outside are buried? There are many plausible explanations.

The first reason, as any animal scientist will tell you, is that prey animals hate change: they like their environment to remain predictable so they can keep out of danger, while predator animals (like dogs and wolves) relish new environments and environmental conditions because they provide more opportunities and resources. However, for a well-fed domesticated dog, this vestigial explanation can't be the whole story, since their wellbeing doesn't depend on hunting or scavenging for food.

New smells

Another explanation is the change in sensory characteristics. Dogs interpret their world mainly through smell; snow changes the olfactory landscape and makes familiar surroundings more challenging and interesting. The boring old back yard becomes a wonderland, fresh for exploration. Essentially, this is one of the same reasons snow appeals to humans – it changes our perspective and makes us interact with our surroundings with renewed attention.

Finally, don't overlook the most obvious reason for your dog's excitement: your own! If there are children in the house, your dog will quickly sense the party atmosphere and want to join in. If he's seen snow before he will remember that snow means a day of play and fun human interaction.

Reverse SNEEZING

THIS LOUD SNORTING SOUNDS MORE LIKE SNORING THAN SNEEZING AND CAN BE QUITE ALARMING WHEN YOU HEAR IT FOR THE FIRST TIME, BUT REVERSE SNEEZING IS USUALLY THE DOG'S INVOLUNTARY REACTION TO MUCUS OR SOME OTHER IRRITANT IN THE NASAL PASSAGE.

It's the reverse of a normal sneeze: the head goes backwards, the mouth closes and air is rapidly sucked into the nose to remove irritants in the area behind the nostrils.

Reverse sneezing is not a medical emergency and it usually stops when the foreign matter is removed, but it could indicate more serious medical problems, so if your dog frequently reverse sneezes, take her to the vet. Any dog can reverse sneeze but it is more commonly associated with breeds with flattened noses (brachycephalic skulls) like Pugs, Boxers and Bulldogs. It often occurs while the dog is asleep or immediately after a long nap, but it can happen at any time.

Although it may distress and perplex your dog, reverse sneezing isn't harmful and most animals return to normal breathing with no ill effects. You can sometimes stop the sneezing by pinching the dog's nose and scratching her throat, or lightly blowing in her face. This will make her swallow and break the sneezing cycle but you only need to do this if the episode doesn't appear to be stopping naturally and she is becoming distressed. The sneeze does, after all, serve an important function of removing foreign matter, but chronic or allergy-related bouts will be more severe, so keep her calm by gently rubbing her sides and back and when it eventually stops, visit the vet at the earliest opportunity.

GUARDING
Furniture

IF YOUR DOG JUMPS ONTO THE SOFA OR A BED,
WINDOWSILL OR ANY SURFACE (USUALLY RAISED)
AND THEN GROWLS AT YOU WHEN YOU GO NEAR,
HE IS TELLING YOU THAT IT BELONGS TO HIM. WHY?
BECAUSE HE THINKS HE'S THE BOSS. WHY?
BECAUSE YOU HAVE ALLOWED HIM TO THINK
THIS BY BEING A WEAK PACK LEADER.

Small dogs

Little dogs are especially prone to this behaviour, but regardless of the size of your dog, it's your responsibility to make him understand that he ranks below the humans in the household. This may seem mean from your perspective. He's your friend and you treat your friends as equals. But you'd be wrong and cruel to apply this principle to your dog. If you want a happy, well-adjusted dog, you have to be the boss, and in fact the dog will appreciate this: the vast majority of dogs don't even want to lead because it's a big responsibility.

On the floor

If he displays this guarding behaviour he must stay on the floor at all times until he learns that you decide where he can go. After a few weeks you can invite him back onto a sofa or bed but only on your terms. If he jumps up without your permission or starts becoming territorial again, send him back to the floor.

Unfortunately, if you have more than one dog and see this behaviour in one of them, then they must all be treated the same and be banned from sofas and beds until you can re-establish yourself as pack leader. Do not ever indulge this guarding behaviour. You own everything in the house – even the dog's bed and toys. You decide when his blanket needs a wash, or when his bed gets moved so you can vacuum behind it.

GROWLING
While Playing

IT IS NORMAL FOR DOGS TO GROWL WHILE THEY PLAY, EITHER WITH YOU OR OTHER DOGS. IT'S ONE OF THE WAYS THEY COMMUNICATE THEIR EMOTIONS. IT SEEMS AGGRESSIVE, BUT IN THE CONTEXT OF PLAY IT IS HARMLESS.

Consider that when dogs rough-house together in play they use all the same moves as in a real fight, such as neck and face biting, pinning to the ground, chasing, body slams, mounting and boxing and even baring teeth, but the activity will have been initiated by a play bow that makes it clear to both participants that it is play. Also you may see exaggerated bouncy movements while they are chasing.

Encourage play fighting

So when your dog growls at you during a tug of war game, she isn't overstepping a boundary, nor is she trying to challenge your place as pack leader. The activity takes place within a framework of play. If you closely watch two dogs play fighting, you'll often see one dog perform a play bow immediately before a particularly rough move like a neck bite or body slam, as a quick reminder that it is still all in good humour.

Do not discourage play fighting. It's a great way for dogs to make friends and learn important social skills, and it builds confidence when they meet strange dogs for the first time. This play rarely escalates into a real dog fight, no matter how aggressive it seems to an onlooker. There should be roughly a 50/50 exchange of roles, rather than one dog always being chased or pinned to the ground, but even this rule can be ignored if the dogs know each other well and unmistakably enjoy each other's company.

Eating GRASS

GRASS EATING IS A VERY COMMON CANINE BEHAVIOUR BUT ITS PURPOSE REMAINS INCONCLUSIVE.

Most dog owners have a vague notion that dogs eat grass to make themselves vomit, but the reality contradicts this homespun wisdom. Less than a quarter of dogs vomit after eating grass, so vets offer a variety of explanations from self-medication for an upset tummy to nutritional deficiencies or plain boredom.

If your dog regularly eats grass, consider if this behaviour coincides with times when he has had less attention or fewer walks. Some experts believe that dogs eat grass to compensate for nutritional deficiencies such as fibre, although they lack the enzymes to digest it, so the nutritional benefit is negligible. Nevertheless, some owners find it stops after switching their dog to a high-fibre diet.

Grass eating occurs in wild canine species such as wolves, where it is thought to combat intestinal parasites. Most domestic dogs are parasite free, especially those who are regularly dewormed, but it is possible that they retain this residual behaviour from their wild ancestors.

Ultimately, it's quite possible that dogs eat grass because they enjoy the texture and the taste. Providing a new chew toy, more exercise, or a more reliable exercise routine can also reduce grass eating. Most vets consider the behaviour normal and harmless so long as it doesn't become obsessive and the grass contains no harmful pesticides.

Burying
BONES

DOGS LIKE TO BURY THINGS. YOU MIGHT THINK YOUR DOG IS DIFFERENT, SINCE YOU'VE NEVER SEEN HER DIGGING A HOLE IN THE BACK GARDEN.

But why do you think so many of her toys, your socks and the remote control work their way underneath the sofa? Coincidence, or the result of your dog's natural urge to protect scarce resources from other predators or members of her own pack, or to hoard a surplus?

For your dog's distant ancestors, burying food used to be necessary for survival, so the burying trait has passed down the generations. At times when competition for food was intense, burying part of the kill would protect it from being stolen by competing carnivores. During times of plenty, excess food would be buried to keep it cool and preserved. The soil would help to disguise the smell of the fresh meat as well as providing natural refrigeration.

Hoarding

Dogs aren't the only creatures who hoard. Squirrels and chipmunks are synonymous with this activity, moles store earthworms in mounds and the jaguar hangs his partially eaten prey high in a tree.

Sometimes too much choice can be counterproductive. If your dog buries food it's because she has plenty and wants to save some for later. If she starts burying or hiding your belongings, she may be asking for more attention. If she stuffs lots of toys in a hiding place, it means she has too many, so it's a good idea to give her fewer toys and rotate them regularly so she doesn't get bored with the glut.

Smelling Like A
WET DOG

DOGS HAVE A UNIQUE ODOUR WHEN THEY ARE
WET. IT'S DIFFICULT TO DESCRIBE BUT EVERYONE
KNOWS WHAT YOU MEAN WHEN YOU SAY 'WET
DOG SMELL'. BUT WHY DO WET DOGS ALL HAVE
THE SAME WET DOG SMELL? WHAT IS IT?

All dogs have microorganisms such as bacteria and yeast
living in their fur, which excrete a range of volatile organic
compounds. Before you turn up your nose, don't forget
that humans are also liberally sprinkled with bacteria.

As you would expect, the bacterial faeces don't smell of
much when dry, but when the dog gets wet the faeces are
broken down by the water, and molecules of chemicals
such as benzaldehyde (almonds), phenylacetaldehyde
(floral/honey), acetaldehyde (fruity/musty), phenol
(medicinal), and 2-methylbutanal (nutty) are released into
the air. The smell of these compounds is greater when the
dog is wet because as the water evaporates from the fur

it carries the smelly molecules into the air like a fine mist. If your dog rubs himself on surfaces inside your house while he is wet, the chemicals will transfer onto them and linger, making your house smell of dog (you won't be able to smell it, but your guests will). The cheapest way to eliminate these smells is to spray and wipe down non-porous surfaces with equal parts apple cider vinegar and water. Carpets and upholstery can be cleaned by sprinkling on a little baking soda: work it in with a soft dry brush, leave for several minutes to allow the baking soda to absorb the odours, and then vacuum clean.

HATING Thunderstorms

WHY DOES THUNDER AND LIGHTNING SCARE SOME DOGS AND NOT OTHERS?

Working and sporting dogs are more prone to storm phobia than other breeds, but thunderstorms bring with them a complex tangle of smells, sights and sounds.

A thunderstorm isn't just loud noise and the occasional flash; it is accompanied by a selection of other atmospheric conditions, any one of which could trigger a sensitive reaction in your dog. Thunderstorms occur when electrical charges build up in clouds, with positively charged ice crystals moving upward toward the top of the clouds and the denser particles at the bottom, which become negatively charged. The negative charge at the base results in a corresponding positive charge on the ground below and when the electrical connection is made between the ground and the cloud the opposing charges equalize and generate a flash of light and heat, expanding the surrounding air to create a supersonic shockwave – the thunder.

Static

Long before the thunder rumbles, your dog will be feeling the environmental effects. She may experience a build-up of static electricity on her fur (which is why some dogs inadvertently earth themselves by lying next to the radiator, or squeezing underneath a metal bed). Even when the storm is some way away, she will be able to smell the nitrogen oxides generated by the storm as well as the

ozone (three molecules of oxygen which bond together after the lightning splits oxygen and nitrogen molecules in the atmosphere).

Sensing your fear

She will also sense a different atmosphere within the household – you might be bustling around closing windows, rushing to bring the washing in off the line, or unplugging electrical equipment. If you are nervous in a storm, she will sense your fear. All these factors can combine to create anxiety in your dog before the first clap of thunder even arrives.

Chasing CATS

DOGS CHASE CATS FOR TWO REASONS: EITHER THEY ARE ACTING AS PREDATORS AND INTEND TO INFLICT SERIOUS DAMAGE ON THE CAT, OR THEY ARE BEHAVING PLAYFULLY AND WANT TO HAVE SOME KNOCKABOUT FUN WITH THEIR FELINE COMPANION.

Dogs are hunters so they catch their prey by chasing, which is why many dogs enjoy chasing after a ball – it is small and travels quickly, triggering the residual chasing/hunting instinct. Cats are also small and travel quickly, so it's easy to see the attraction.

Whatever the motive, it's your job as a responsible owner to make sure that all cat bothering is anticipated and avoided. Even if you think you know that your dog is 'harmless' and is having fun, you should always prioritize the welfare of both animals. Dogs and cats can easily get injured while they chase and flee, especially if they run into traffic.

Even being chased by a 'friendly' playful dog is very stressful for the cat, because it has no way of guessing the dog's intentions. A playful dog can injure a cat by playing too aggressively, so the moment you spot a cat nearby, call your dog to you and put him on a leash until you have passed by. If he is already on the leash don't let him sprint off in pursuit because when he reaches the end of the leash the snap stop can damage his vertebrae. Distract him away from the cat with a treat or change of direction and walk calmly past.

Walking In Circles Before LYING DOWN

EVEN THOUGH OUR DOGS TODAY SLEEP IN
CUSHIONED DOGGY BASKETS, ON OUR BEDS,
ON CARPETS OR LAMINATE FLOORS,
IT WASN'T ALWAYS THIS WAY.

Before they were domesticated and probably for thousands of years after they formed a special relationship with humans, dogs had to make their own beds every night by flattening vegetation, sand or snow before hunkering down for the night.

This circling ritual would have got rid of snakes and large insects, created a soft, level surface and would also have sent out a visible marker to other dogs that the territory had been reserved. Those genetic traits still remain in our modern domesticated animals even though they are redundant.

Other theories

Some dogs have a good scratch around their bedding too, which is also ancestral behaviour from when they had to dig sleeping hollows either to keep cool in hot conditions by lying in the cool soil, or to retain body heat in cooler climes. Another theory suggests that dogs like to sleep with their nose into the wind, so they circle to determine the wind direction.

Some experts claim that dogs that are on high alert, such as the guarding breeds, spend longer than average circling and settling themselves and that this gives them the opportunity to survey their surroundings while they wind down and mentally clock off duty.

Discomfort

Although circling is common, and can usually be regarded as normal behaviour, if your dog circles excessively before settling down, she may have neurological problems or be suffering pain from a physical condition such as arthritis. If she remains restless and can't seem to settle, despite lots of circling and digging, take her to the vet for a check-up.

FOLLOWING
Me Everywhere

YOUR DOG LOVES YOU. YOU ARE HIS WHOLE WORLD. WHEN YOU GO AWAY HE FEELS ANXIOUS AND LOOKS FORWARD TO YOUR RETURN. SO IT MAKES PERFECT SENSE THAT HE WOULD WANT TO FOLLOW YOU AROUND WHEN YOU WALK THROUGH THE FRONT DOOR AND BACK INTO HIS LIFE.

However, following can easily tip over into stalking and it can be irritating and guilt-inducing to find you've created a Velcro mutt.

If your dog is following you too much for comfort, you need to adopt some predictable routines that can reduce his anxiety and give him some anchors, so he feels more stable. Dogs like routine. Make sure he gets at least thirty minutes of exercise (and preferably more) at the same time each day. If you skip a walk you only have yourself to blame when his anxiety levels increase because he hasn't burned off excess energy. Also, establish fixed times for play, feeding and training.

The more familiar your dog becomes with the predictable, enjoyable timetable of his day, the more he will relax. It is also very important to create a stable and calm home environment. If you are constantly arguing with your partner or your children, your dog will pick up on the tension and become very anxious.

Surprisingly, the fact that your dog follows you around does not necessarily mean that he considers you the pack leader (that might be someone else in your household). Studies of dog behaviour in packs show that they are more likely to follow the friendliest dog rather than the alpha. So the plus side of your dog's possible anxiety is that he feels very safe in your esteemed company.

Acting As If It's Constantly
HUNGRY

SOMETIMES YOU CAN START TO WONDER WHETHER YOU ARE FEEDING YOUR DOG ENOUGH OR WHETHER SHE IS GETTING ALL HER ESSENTIAL NUTRIENTS.

These nagging doubts begin to surface when you're in the kitchen preparing or eating your own food and you suddenly become aware that once again you have become prime-time viewing for your doe-eyed hungry pooch. So how do you know if she is genuinely hungry or just trying to guilt-trip you into tossing her a tasty human morsel?

Dog food

If you follow the guidelines on your dog food packaging then you will be feeding more than enough. Dog food manufacturers want you to buy as much of their product as possible, so they recommend large portions. So long as the food is a good quality complete balanced diet and you haven't recently increased her level of daily exercise, you can be confident that your dog, like most, is simply a greedy guts who will eat whatever is put in front of her. If you have more than one dog it's worth keeping an eye on feeding time to make sure no one is having more than their fair share, and depriving another dog in the process.

In rare cases, however, she might be eternally hungry because she has diabetes or hyperthyroidism. If you are worried, ask a vet to perform a blood test.

Weight

To check if your dog is a healthy weight, view from above and the waist should taper in before the hind legs. In side profile, your dog's belly should also tuck in. If it sticks out, she's overweight. You should be able to feel her ribs, but not see them (although in some breeds, such as Greyhounds, visible ribs are acceptable).

So why is your dog always hungry? She probably isn't, but she won't pass up a tasty snack, because her ancestors never knew when their next meal would be, and she retains their instinct to graze whenever the opportunity arises.

JUMPING
Up On People

DOGS JUMP UP TO GREET HUMANS BECAUSE
WE ARE TALLER THAN THEM AND THEY WANT
TO GREET US THE SAME WAY THEY GREET OTHER
DOGS – BY SNIFFING OUR FACES. SO WHEN A
DOG JUMPS UP HE IS ACTING INSTINCTIVELY
RATHER THAN BEING NAUGHTY.

However, even if you enjoy being pounced on by your furry friends, for the sake of other people you should teach him that you only pay attention to dogs who keep all four paws on the ground.

Actions, as always, speak louder than words, so shouting 'down' is less effective than simply ignoring him until he puts his front feet on the floor. As soon as he performs the desired behaviour, give him your full attention and lots of praise. He will quickly learn that jumping up is a waste of time and achieves worse than nothing because it delays the greeting.

So, the next time you come home, if he jumps up, don't speak or even push him away. Keep your hands by your side, stand up straight and ignore him. If he keeps jumping up, turn away and stay quiet, no matter how frustrated you feel. Any reaction from you at this stage, even a negative one, is a reward. Your dog will have to return to earth at some point – be alert and praise immediately. He'll soon begin to associate four paws on the ground with happy outcomes and stop jumping up.

Wagging Its
TAIL

IT IS A COMMON MISCONCEPTION THAT DOGS WAG THEIR TAILS TO SHOW THAT THEY ARE HAPPY AND FRIENDLY – THE LANGUAGE OF A DOG'S TAIL IS MUCH MORE SUBTLE AND EXPRESSIVE. DOGS CAN CONVEY A RANGE OF EMOTIONS AND SOCIAL SIGNALS WITH THEIR TAILS INCLUDING FEAR, HAPPINESS, STATUS AND AGGRESSION.

Animal scientists provide increasingly sophisticated interpretations of tail gestures. The latest research shows that dogs wag their tails more to the right when they are happy and more to the left when they are sad or uncertain. Other dogs can read this information. Neuroscientists at the University of Trento, Italy, monitored the heart rates of 43 dogs while they were shown a video of another dog wagging its tail or sitting still. The heart rate increased and they showed other signs of stress such as turning their heads away when viewing dogs whose tails wagged to the left.

The height of the tail is also important. When the tail is held high, the dog feels confident and dominant (also a sign of aggression when challenged, so back off); when the tail is horizontal the dog is attentive and alert; the tail drops low and between the legs in response to anxiety and fear and indicates submission.

The width and speed of the wag also conveys important information. When dogs meet for the first time they usually offer either a tentative narrow wag or a broad friendly non-threatening wag; if the tail is held very high and vibrating with tiny high-speed movements, this is a sign of aggression. When a dog is really excited, happy and friendly, the tail wags in a wide circular motion like a propeller.

Shivering And
SHAKING

THERE ARE AT LEAST SIX COMMON REASONS WHY DOGS SHIVER AND SHAKE, ONLY SOME OF WHICH REQUIRE MEDICAL ATTENTION.

First of all, it's important to distinguish shivering and shaking from a seizure, in which the dog's body convulses and jerks and the legs paddle involuntarily.

The primary cause of shaking is excitement. If your dog is prone to excited shivering, the mere mention of walkies can be enough to set them off. Some breeds accompany this with a plaintive moaning whine that sounds like they are crying with excitement. This is caused by adrenaline and is perfectly normal.

The second most likely cause of shivering, especially in small dogs, is cold. A dog's normal body temperature is nearly four degrees higher than ours, so you won't necessarily be able to tell just by touch. You need to be super vigilant during the winter months.

Dogs also shiver when they are scared. A sudden loud noise, fireworks, a strange environment or an aggressive dog can all provoke a shivering response. If you can't remove your dog from the stimulus, try to soothe him with a calming tone of voice.

Shivering can also be a learned behaviour that has been rewarded in the past by human attention so the dog has realized that he can get attention at will by turning on the shakes.

Problems

While much shivering is harmless, it can in some cases indicate neurological or muscular problems, especially in older dogs. If your dog starts to shake when he wasn't previously prone to doing so, or if you suspect that he is shivering because of pain, see your vet.

Finally, shivering can be a sign of poisoning and it can occur very quickly after the animal has ingested a toxin (within minutes). If your dog is shaking for none of the reasons above, do not delay. Race him to the vet immediately so he can be given an emetic (or anti-venom in the case of a snakebite) because the longer the toxin remains in his body, the lower his chance of survival.

SMELLING
The Morning Air

IF YOU'VE EVER OBSERVED YOUR DOG WHEN
YOU FIRST LET HER OUT INTO THE BACK GARDEN
YOU'LL SOMETIMES SEE HER STAND STILL,
NECK STRETCHED, HEAD RAISED HIGH TO
DRINK IN THE CRISP MORNING AIR.

She may even curl back her upper lip to expose her front
teeth and hold this position for a few seconds. This is a

specialized type of super-smelling called the Flehmen response.

Dogs have about 250 million olfactory receptor cells in their noses, while humans have a mere 5 million. Furthermore, the area of a dog's brain dedicated to processing smells takes up more relative brain area. These two factors make it possible for dogs' sense of smell to be up to 100,000 times more sensitive than ours. So dogs interpret the world mainly through this important sense.

They can even smell different smells in each nostril at the same time and in common with many animals, they have a 'Jacobson's organ' (aka the vomeronasal organ or VNO), which is mainly used to detect pheromones: chemical messengers that are secreted in sweat, excreta and other bodily fluids. This organ helps to process the olfactory information during the Flehmen response. So when your dog sniffs the air it's like speed-reading the morning newspaper. She can learn masses of information about her surroundings, such as the presence of other animals, including humans, and check that all is right with the world. After this important job is complete, she might come inside and have a well-earned lie down.

Barking At
'NOTHING'

YOU'VE JUST DRAGGED YOURSELF OUT OF YOUR COMFY CHAIR AND TRUDGED TO THE FRONT DOOR FOR THE FOURTH TIME. YOU KNOW THERE'S NOTHING THERE BUT YOUR DOG WON'T STOP BARKING, SEEMINGLY AT ABSOLUTELY NOTHING.

So what's really going on? Are you reinforcing the behaviour by responding to the bark alarm, is there something outside that you're missing, or is he barking for a completely different reason?

Better hearing

Dogs have much better hearing than us, so common sense tells you to check for an external cause for the barking. If you can't locate it, your dog may be responding to a sound that has nothing to do with your property (he may have heard a howl that is half a mile away). It's also possible that he's barking at something he saw but you didn't – like a squirrel running up a tree – but it is equally likely that he is barking because he feels anxious or bored. Distract him with a bone or chew toy and see if the behaviour persists.

Don't scold or shout as this will only reinforce the unwanted behaviour because he will think you're joining in; it will also increase his anxiety, making him even more prone to bark.

Compulsive Barking

If your dog really is a compulsive barker who drives you mad with his incessant barking at nothing, he will usually exhibit other repetitive behaviours such as pacing up and down or in a circle or running to a particular spot. It's worth talking to your vet, firstly to rule out any medical problems, and secondly because they will be able to help you with specific training to reduce your dog's anxiety and to show you how to be a more effective pack leader.

The more often you can reassure your dog that you have taken responsibility for whatever has caused him to bark, the sooner he can step down from high alert, confident that you will deal with the perceived threat.

Eating TISSUES

TISSUE MUNCHING IS A VERY COMMON CANINE FASCINATION. YOU MIGHT BE SURPRISED TO LEARN THE REAL REASON WHY DOGS STEAL TISSUES, TEAR THEM APART AND SOMETIMES SWALLOW THEM – AND IT ISN'T ANYTHING TO DO WITH EATING.

They have no nutritional value and even used ones aren't very tasty; there is some pleasure to be had in ripping them up, but the overwhelming reason for this behaviour is attention seeking.

And boy does it get your attention, especially when shreds of tissue are spread all over the lounge. As any dog owner knows, picking up all those little pieces is a back-breaking and time-consuming chore. So your reaction is naturally negative – you might chase the dog and snatch back the tissue before she makes a mess, or call the dog to you when you discover the litter all over the floor. Either way,

she gets your attention, and it doesn't matter that the attention is negative. It still rewards and reinforces the unwanted behaviour.

If your dog only steals one or two tissues, you can stop the behaviour by ignoring her whenever it happens – withdraw your attention, avert your eyes, don't look at her and carry on with whatever you were doing. Tidy up any mess when she has left the room and don't shout or curse while doing it! If the tissue eating gains no attention from you it will stop within a few weeks. It may get worse first as she escalates the behaviour to provoke a response – this is called an 'extinction burst' and it's a good sign as it means your ignoring her is working.

Moving Food From The
BOWL
Before Eating

IT CAN BE FRUSTRATING TO WATCH AS YOUR DOG REMOVES FOOD FROM HIS SHINY NEW STAINLESS STEEL FEEDING BOWL, CARRIES IT AWAY, THEN DROPS IT ON THE FLOOR AND TUCKS INTO THE MORSELS BEFORE RETURNING FOR ANOTHER MOUTHFUL.

Not only does this curious dining ritual seem inefficient, it makes a mess. Actually the reason is relatively straight-forward.

In the wild prey animals have a pecking order when eating their kill. The dominant animals receive 'the lion's share' and the choicest cuts, while the subordinate members of the pack either content themselves with the leftovers or take some food from the carcass and move away from the other animals to avoid possible conflict.

If your dog moves food from the bowl he was probably one of the subordinate members of the litter and may continue this behaviour well into adulthood. Remember that you are part of his new pack, so he may be moving the food away from you. Leave the area so he can eat in peace, and if there are other dogs, feed them in separate areas of the room or house. Subordinate dogs will also eat quickly because when there is competition for food eating quickly is important for survival and to get the maximum nutrition before being chased away by a more dominant member of the pack.

BARKING
At The Vacuum Cleaner

THERE ARE AT LEAST THREE SOLID REASONS WHY YOUR DOG MIGHT BE FRIGHTENED OF THE VACUUM CLEANER.

It's big, it's noisy and possibly most disconcerting of all, every time it appears you seem to be fighting with it, as it drags you erratically back and forth across every room

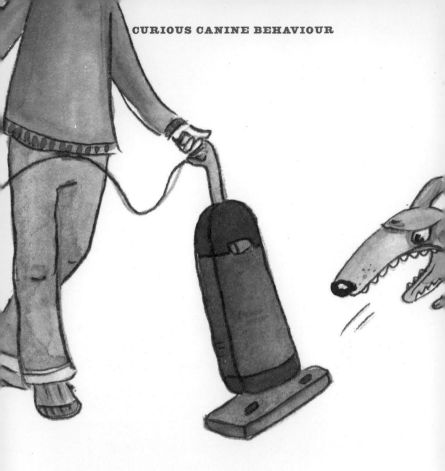

in the house. From your dog's point of view, once a week you get beaten up by a huge screaming plastic monster. No wonder you keep it in that scary cupboard. It's a threat to everybody's sanity.

Treat

You can teach your dog to be comfortable around the vacuum cleaner by using treats and conditioning. First place the vacuum in the middle of the room and reward her with a treat every time she plucks up the courage to go near it and give it a sniff. Soon she will associate going close to the vacuum with receiving treats. Next begin to move it gently around and keep rewarding her calm behaviour.

Distraction

Next switch the stationary cleaner on and off rapidly and treat her immediately so she is distracted by the treat rather than the sound. Then leave the vacuum on and treat her as long as she is not reacting. If she freaks out, go back a step and consolidate before moving forward. Finally, switch on the vacuum and move it around the room, treating your dog frequently for staying calm. Repeat this training once a week and pretty soon she'll be salivating every time you go near that scary cupboard of horrors.

Preferring A HARD FLOOR To A SOFT BED

IF YOUR DOG REFUSES TO SLEEP IN HIS BED OR ON YOUR BED BUT PREFERS TO SPEND MOST OF THE NIGHT ON A HARD COLD FLOOR, YOU'RE NOT ALONE.

Many dogs like their own bed because it is the only part of the house that is truly theirs and that usually no other member of the 'pack' uses (apart from the occasional curious toddler), but many seem to spend as little time in their bed as possible.

It might look uncomfortable and make you feel guilty that there's something wrong with your dog's bed, but there's no need to worry about his apparent ascetic choices. Dogs are always looking for the easy life, so if he prefers a hard floor it's probably because he overheats with fabric bedding and prefers the cool tiles or laminate.

Keep the bed

Even though he favours the floor, and rarely uses his bed, don't get rid of it. As he gets older he may enjoy the comfort of a softer sleeping place as his bones become more brittle or arthritic, especially if he's a larger dog, because they have more weight to put pressure on their skeleton.

Wherever they sleep, dogs need relatively firm support, so a soft, super-squidgy surface is unsuitable. The most comfortable places in the house will probably be the sofa and your bed, but dogs can develop joint problems in later life from jumping on and off these surfaces if they are too high up, so be vigilant if he's small or a developing puppy.

Bringing Me Its
BLANKET

MANY DOG OWNERS EXPERIENCE A VOLLEY OF GIFT GIVING WHEN THEY RETURN HOME. YOUR DOG PROBABLY GREETS YOU AT THE THRESHOLD AND THEN TEARS OFF TO FIND A BONE, BLANKET, SHOE OR SOCK TO PRESENT IN HONOUR OF YOUR ARRIVAL.

However, this is more than a simple display of affection or even submission. It is actually quite a sophisticated use of body language.

When you get home your dog becomes highly aroused and excited. She wants to jump all over you but this is bad manners in dog communities as well as in human interaction, so she displaces some of this energy by retrieving a toy. This allows her to focus some of her excess energy into the object, rather than allow herself to breach etiquette and throw herself on you, which could be interpreted as aggressive. In fact, most owners instinctively discourage this kind of greeting and would push their dog away. Bringing a toy or blanket introduces an element of play into the greeting.

Sometimes the play element is made even more explicit, when she does a play bow and then drags the blanket outside. She is inviting you to chase or play tug of war.

We subsequently reinforce this gift giving with praise and attention because we find it cute and enjoyable, so the dog gets the message loud and clear that a blanket or favourite toy is de rigueur in all future welcoming ceremonies.

Licking ME

DOGS LICK FOR A VARIETY OF REASONS AND IT IS A NATURAL PART OF DOG COMMUNICATION AND BEHAVIOUR; IT FEELS AND TASTES GOOD AND YOUR DOG HAS LEARNED THAT HE GETS MORE ATTENTION WHEN HE LICKS YOU.

A mother licks her puppies to keep them clean and puppies quickly incorporate this grooming behaviour into their own routine. Littermates will lick each other to strengthen bonds and also for mutual benefit, cleaning those hard to reach places. So from the earliest age dogs associate licking with pleasure, bonding, grooming and feeding.

Face licking

In the wild puppies will gather round the mother when she returns from a hunting trip and lick her face. This looks like an affectionate greeting but it has a more practical function in terms of survival: it stimulates the mother's regurgitation reflex, so she hocks up some partially digested prey, which is ideal for her developing brood. Domestic dogs retain this regurgitation reflex, although it is much weaker, so it is rare to see mother dogs regurgitating for their puppies if they are well looked after.

Face licking is also a sign of deference or submissiveness to a more dominant dog, to demonstrate that the dog doing the licking is not a threat. When this occurs, the submissive dog will often lower its body, while the dominant dog will stand tall and receive its due, without reciprocation.

Communication

When your dog licks your face he could be greeting you (watch out for those licks when you return home), asking for a treat ('Sick me up a biscuit please') or communicating submission ('I need you'). A longer licking session, on your forearm for example, is linked to grooming behaviour, although the saltiness of your skin is a never-ending source of pleasure.